JESUS CHRIST IS FOR REAL

JOHN GHIRONTE

WESTBOW
PRESS®
A DIVISION OF THOMAS NELSON
& ZONDERVAN

WestBow Press books may be ordered through booksellers or by contacting:

WestBow Press
A Division of Thomas Nelson & Zondervan
1663 Liberty Drive
Bloomington, IN 47403
www.westbowpress.com
844-714-3454

Scripture taken from the NEW AMERICAN STANDARD BIBLE®, Copyright © 1960, 1962, 1963, 1968, 1971, 1972, 1973, 1975, 1977, 1995 by The Lockman Foundation. Used by permission. www.Lockman.org

ISBN: 978-1-6642-2914-3 (sc)
ISBN: 978-1-6642-2913-6 (e)

Library of Congress Control Number: 2021906415

Print information available on the last page.

WestBow Press rev. date: 08/05/2021

I feel mournful writing this memoir. My mom just passed away on Saturday morning at four o'clock, New Year's Day. She was eighty-one years of age. I know that she's in a better place. I will write about this in my last chapter, letting everyone know that there is life after death for everyone who believes in the Father, Jesus Christ. Amen. I never got around to writing this book before as I've been busy working two jobs and taking care of my family the best I can. But this time, with my mom passing, I went to the store, bought a notebook and a couple of pencils, and started writing.

My name is Ionel John Ghironte, and I was born in Adjud, Romania, on May 8, 1965, the son of Alixandru Ghironte and Aneta Hanga. I dearly love my sister, Lenuta, and brother, Alexandru. I was told that before I was born, life was pretty harsh. Both my parents were farmers, but my dad had it worse. He was ill, suffering from tuberculosis (TB) and spending a lot of time in the hospital, leaving my mom alone with two children and all the work that needed to be done to survive. Imagine. It was rough.

When I was thirteen or fourteen, my mom told me that when she got pregnant with me, my dad wanted me aborted. I imagine that he could not afford another mouth to feed, being in their situation. Of course she had abortions before; it was very common at the time. My father sent her to the hospital to take care of it. But when Mom went to the hospital and spoke to the doctor, he told her it was too late to do it. I think my mom was relieved because she didn't want an abortion. She told me that I was moving in her belly and kicking hard at the time. I believe that was a sign from God to spare my life. So my mom went home and told my father that she could not do it. Not with this baby. I think my dad was disappointed, but I know that my dad was not a bad person. He was just worried about her and how he couldn't be there for the two children they already had. Then after a while, he got over it. I think in his heart he did not want to do it either. I know that would be a hard decision to make for everyone, no matter what the circumstances. After all, we are all humans.

A few months later came the time to give birth in Corbasca, the village where we were living. But there were complications with me. My umbilical cord was wrapped around my neck, making it difficult for me to breathe. So they had to rush my mom to the hospital in Adjud, which was about eleven to fourteen kilometers away, in order to give birth safely. Finally, after many hours of struggling, I was born with the umbilical cord still wrapped around my neck. My mom told me that when she saw me, my face was purple due to the lack of oxygen, and I had a big red spot on my left cheek. They all wondered why that red spot was there, but Mom did not care as long I was alive and healthy.

That spot went away before I reached three or four years of age. Some say that I was murdered in my previous life, resulting in that red mark. Who knows? It may be true if you believe in reincarnation.

I don't know what my dad said when he first saw me, but I think he was proud of me, just like any father would be. He was spending most of his time in the hospital for treatment and some time with us at home. My dad told my mom after a while, "Wife, you should never tell this boy that I told you to abort him. Because if you do, I will always curse you, even after my death." So you see, deep in his heart, he did not want to do it either.

My dad was a cowboy. He was very good with animals. He was a tall, handsome man and well-spoken and skinny just like me. I remember people from my neighborhood telling me that I looked just like him, but I think I look more like my mother's side, with blond hair and brown eyes. Unlike my brother and sister, who have dark hair and dark eyes. That's why my father used to call me, "My little Jewish son." Jews were well known as having blond hair in my country.

I don't have a lot of memories about my father. He passed away when I was seven years old, when he was forty-one. I was told that my father went to a wedding for one of his friends. He drank too much that day, and being tired, he slept outside on a haystack. It was very cold that night, so he got sick and caught pneumonia. If he had been treated in time, he could've lived many years. But unfortunately, he did not.

He finally did go to the hospital, but the pneumonia was too far advanced. The doctor kept him on medication to prolong his life for several more years, but the TB was too far spread, and it caused his death. The last time I saw him was when he left the house in an ambulance. I was playing outside, climbing on a fence, when I saw him leave. My dad told Mom that would be the last time they would see each other, that he would come home dead. He knew that his chances were slim, and he was right.

I suppose that when the time to die is near, you somehow know. May his soul rest in peace. My dad is the guy in the white shirt.

One of the memories of my dad was when he was sitting on a rock near my grandparents' house. In front of the house was a flower patch. It was very beautiful, and I was playing in the middle of it. Dad was watching me all the time, and he kept calling, "Come to Daddy! Come to Daddy!" But I did not want to go to him because I was afraid of him. Then he took me in his arms and started kissing and hugging me. Thinking that he may not have a lot of time to spend with me must've been stressful for him. I also remember seeing him on a stack of firewood, with his face resting in his palms and looking very sad.

Everybody knew everybody in the neighborhood where I was raised. Laidback people, boys being boys, we played outside. One guy was older than me by seven or eight years. He was kind of crazy. I think I was two to three years old and must've said something wrong to him, which he didn't like. I ran, and he caught me. Then he tied the straps of my pants around my neck pretty tight and sent me home.

At the time, no one was home, so I lay down on the doorstep and fell asleep. Luckily, my mom was on her way home and saw me lying there, unconscious and barely breathing, and she somehow got hold of my father. He was really mad as he took his pocketknife and cut the straps so I could breathe. She told me later, when I was older, that I could have died in a matter of minutes if they hadn't shown up when they did. When Dad asked who did that to me, I told him, "The crazy guy did." My dad went to his house and told the father that his son almost killed me. He apologized continuously to my father. Luckily, the kid ran away. Otherwise, my dad would've hurt him badly.

Dad was also a beekeeper. We had three or four beehives in front of the house. That was a very delicate job. I always enjoyed the honey and watching my father take care of them. When he was collecting the honey, I was always there so I could eat it. He would have huge wooden bowl of honey. I crawled to it, dipped my finger in it, and ate. My dad wasn't too happy about it. He told my mom to keep me away because I could spoil it. She replied that it was okay since I was just a baby. He started smiling.

The honeybees were doing really well over there. We had many fruit trees and flowers, a little vineyard, and acacia trees everywhere. It gives a distinctive flavor to the honey, very sweet and aromatic.

My brother and I got along pretty well. He was three years older than me. He was always eating. He loved to eat, so he was well built and stronger than I was.

To this day, I'm afraid of cows. One time my brother and I went to the pasture with our cow. On that pasture was also a cow that belonged to someone else. He told us not to get too close to her because she could get mean or scared. But I didn't listen to him. I got close so I could see what the cow would do. In a split second, she ran, picked me up between her horns, and threw me into the air, about ten feet high, dropping me into a hazelnut bush. Imagine if that cow had punctured me with her horns. I could've dead on the ground. I got really lucky. When my brother saw this, he grabbed a bat and beat the poor cow.

I t wasn't her fault. It was mine because I did not listen. From then on you will never see me near a cow.

My sister was the oldest one. To tell you the truth, I don't have a lot of memories of her when we were growing up. She was taught at a boarding school in the city. Maybe that's why we didn't spend a lot of time together. I think my first memory of her is when my father passed away. I remember she was dressed in black and was crying. Standing at my father's coffin, she put her palms on his forehead. She was fifteen years old at the time. My brother was next to her, and I was next to him.

At the time I did not realize that my father died. Being only seven years old, I didn't know what it meant to be dead. There were a lot of people at the funeral, friends but mainly relatives. When they were laying him in the ground, people gathered around to see him for the last time. I somehow ended up behind them. Luckily one of the relatives grabbed me and brought me closer, so I could see him one last time. I did not see it then, but when I grew up, I thought, *It must've been very sad.* The previous picture was made several years after my dad's funeral. I is of my brother, my sister, my mom, and me.

being Christian orthodox, things are done differently over there. They unbury the dead after seven years to see the remains and to give thanks to the soul by giving things like food, clothes, sweets, and wine to other people in the deceased's name. In that way, the dead can receive the goods in the afterlife.

After a while, my mom bought some new furniture and a black-and-white TV. I think we were the first ones on that street to buy a TV; it was a big deal back then. A lot of people came to our house to watch the news, but mainly movies and the Olympics. It was 1976, when Nadia Comaneci won the gymnastics in Montreal, Canada. Everyone was so proud of her; I was watching too. But my favorite things to watch were American movies, especially cowboy movies. Everyone was crazy about them, starting from the youngest to the oldest.

I was a little bit older when I first saw the *Dallas* series on TV. My whole house was packed. That was the only series that really made me go to the West. I remember one time my sister and I were working outside in the backyard, and I told her that one day I would go to Dallas for good to live there. She smiled and said that would never be possible. I told her, "We will see about that."

One day my neighbor-friend and I were playing outside near the beehives. We had two big pear trees in front of the house. Being late in the summer, there were not many pears left. I told him I would grab a stick and throw it at the one pear I did find so we could eat it. Sure enough, I hit it, and the pear landed on a beehive. And guess what happened next.

All the bees started flying out and chased us. There must have been hundreds of them. My friend got away faster and ran home with just a few stings on him. But I was in big trouble. I could not climb the stairs to get out of there, and I fell. Bees covered almost half my body. Mom took me in her arms after she wiped them away the best she could and ran to our village doctor. She kept asking me if I was okay and telling me not to fall asleep. I shouted at her, saying I was fine. When we arrived at the doctor, he gave me a shot.

I was scared of him, especially when I saw the needle. I asked him what was in it. He said it was just water, and after an injection, I would be fine. That calmed me down quite a bit.

I don't remember anything more about it. When I got older, my family told me that I was put in dark room in the house, and they prayed for the best. They didn't think I would make it. My face was turning blue and became unrecognizable because of the venom from the beestings. I slowly started recovering. And I know this is strange, but to this day, I have never had a headache. I was thinking and said to many people that it might have been because of the venom of the bees. Come to think of it, in small doses it's actually good for you. Maybe scientists can do some research about it. But in large doses, it can be fatal. I could have died then, and I was really close to it. Let's just say that someone was watching over me.

Being the youngest in the family, I pretty much did most of the chores around the house. My sister told my brother to do whatever needed to be done, and then he would tell me to do it. One time I shouted at him and said that I wasn't going to do it and that he needed to do it himself. Why did I have to do it all the time? We were kids, and I know he didn't mean it, but he got really mad and was playing with a knife. I started running toward the gate, and he threw the knife at me. When I saw the knife flying at me, I made a quick right, so the knife would not hit me. I was quite wrong. The knife was impaled into my back—not all the way, but it got stuck. I was so scared and started screaming. My neighbor heard and rushed through the gate to see what happened. She immediately pulled the knife out and poured some kerosene on the wound. To tell you the truth, the pain went away; it was a quick remedy. Everyone in a household had kerosene as it had multiple uses. My brother tried to calm me and begged me not to tell Mom about it. I, being a good brother, did not, but I think my good neighbor told her what happened. When our mom got home, she rushed into the house, and the first thing she did was to look at my back. I had a small stain of blood. She was so scared that she beat my poor brother with a stick pretty badly. I started laughing, being scared. And she beat me, too, a little bit but not as bad she did my brother. Mom finally calmed down and she said, "I left the two of you alone for a while, and this is what happened. Rascals."

I always remind my brother of this to remind him, and we start laughing. When he tells me, "I could have killed you," I counter with, "No you couldn't. You didn't throw it hard enough." We start laughing and hugging each other. By the way, I still have that scar on my back.

Come to think of it, I could have died so many times in my childhood. I had it pretty rough. But we had some good times, too, playing soccer and tennis. I was very good at tennis.

My favorite was fishing. I had to sneak out of my house to go fishing because my mom wouldn't let me. I always wondered why she wouldn't let me go fishing. Then later I found out that my mother took me to a fortune-teller, who told her that I would travel above a huge body of water, and she was concerned about it. She figured that if I went fishing or near water, I would have died swimming or something might have happened to me. That's why I never learned to swim until I came to America. I know it's pretty weird, but the fortune-teller was right. I indeed traveled on top of big weather, flying over a big ocean in an airplane to come here.

Time passed, and I finished the eighth grade. Then I went to the city for higher education. I was not very good in school. My sister was the smartest one. She was always studying. My brother was pretty smart, too, maybe smarter than me.

I was the black sheep of the family. I barely made it through the first two years of high school because I always skipped school. I always made new friends and went to the movies and played soccer and tennis. But I always showed up for the final exam, sometimes making better grades than the guys who made it to school every day, five days a week. They wondered how I did it, but I didn't in every subject. In the tenth grade I failed big time. I had to repeat the grade if I didn't study hard enough.

I never studied so hard in my life that summer because I had to pass the summer exams in math and physics, my two toughest subjects. I told my mom about it, and she was kind of disappointed. But I promised I would study all summer long and wouldn't let her down. Then the exams came that I had prepared for. Somehow I studied better on physics than math. My math teacher told me if I had studied like that during the school year, I would have been the best in the class. I passed the physics exam too. To tell you the truth, I was kind of proud of myself, making it through with flying colors. My mom was proud of me too.

After I finished tenth grade, I went to the trade school in Bucharest (the capital of Romania) and studied two years to become a machinist. While I studied, I also received hands-on training at Energo-Reparatie, a big factory. I met some good people and made a lot of friends at the factory and at school.

After some time, I started working full time, making a pretty good living. They were paying us cash. It was like that everywhere; there were no payroll checks in Romania. Things started to get boring. You know, home and work, again and again. Then one of my good friends suggested, "Let's check out the whole country." Sure enough, we started skipping work and started places around the country.

It was not that simple, though. Since we did not have much money, we ended up sleeping in the parks and eating fruits most of the time, whatever we could find. But most of all, we started getting in trouble with the authorities. We decided to go back, hoping to get our old jobs back. That didn't happen. They didn't hire us back because we had not been trustworthy. That gave me a good reason to go even further. I didn't have a choice as I had to look for a job in order to survive.

So I went to Drobeta-Turnu-Severin, a city close to the border. We were walking one day to the market, where there were several people from Yugoslavia selling their goods to Romanians. They included blue jeans, sneakers, all kinds of stuff. To own such things was something at the time. While we're looking around, we were arrested by the border patrol. They took us in for interrogation one by one. When I went in, there was a captain (I think) standing in front of a Romanian map. Then he asked me what we were doing over there.

I said we were looking for jobs, and I heard that an underground mine was hiring. He did not believe me. I think he thought we were trying to leave the country, being so close to the border. But he was wrong at the time. I did not want to go because I could not swim. In order to leave illegally, you had to swim the Danube River, and it was too dangerous. I heard a lot of people died doing just that.

T hen aiming at the map, he asked if I knew where Yugoslavia was located on the map. Of course I knew, but I played a fool and told him I didn't know. Then he hit me with a ruler. He got really angry because he knew I was lying.

Then he told me, "If you want to live in the West, you oughta go all over the country to see the beautifulness. Have you done that?" I told him no, I hadn't see all the country, but I was going to when I could find a job. He wasn't dumb; he was trained for interrogation. He knew there was something odd about me, jobless and that close to the border. So he threw us in jail for twenty-four hours. I was very hungry, and they gave us fish and rice, which tasted very good.

When he let us go it was with one condition. When we found jobs, we had to let him know about it. We said we would come back to let him know. But we never did.

Finally, we got jobs working in an underground mine for six to seven months. Working conditions were rough, hard, and dangerous. But we were making a very good living. The pay was high, and I was making twice what I was making as a machinist in Bucharest. I was thinking more and more about leaving—you know, crossing the border. But I had to find a place where I could cross on land. I had better chances doing that than crossing on water.

I worked in the mine with a guy from Resita. The funny part was that he had a red mark on his face, just like I did at the time. I considered him my best friend since we both had the birthmark on our faces, even though mine was faded. His name was Puiu.

Puiu also wanted to go across, so we planned for the next step. Then we decided to go to his hometown to get a job there. Because he used to be employed there at Combinatu Siderurgie-Resita, he could get me in, and he did. They hired me as a bricklayer in a steel factory.

Puiu had another friend who was thinking about going across as well. I met him, talked to him, and said we wanted to go with him. But he turned us down. After a while we heard that he got caught by the border patrol. He got out after a couple of months—I remember it was in August—thanks to a presidential pardon. When we saw him, he did not talk a lot as he was beaten pretty badly.

You have to know this: When they catch you, they will beat you really badly. You are lucky if they let you out alive. Puiu's friend was really scared. We told him we were going to go and asked him to join us. He said, "If they catch you, they will kill you or beat you up so bad that you cannot walk up straight. I'm the proof of that."

Not only did he not want to go with us anymore, my "good buddy" was giving up, too, because he had doubts. "I don't know, man. It's pretty scary. What if we get caught? What if we end up worse than him? I cannot take that chance."

I told Puiu, "Fine. I'm going to go by myself then. If they catch me, so be it. But I'm taking that chance."

In the meantime, I received order papers to join the army. In those days, Romania, being a communist country, you had to go in the army whether you liked it or not; it was an obligation. I got called into the office for a meeting. The guy looked at me, measuring me up and down. He told me he had trouble locating me for some time. I was indeed running from army recruiters because I didn't want to join them at all. My dream was to leave for the West as soon as possible. I didn't want to live in Romania anymore.

He started writing on the application, telling me that I was going to like this, and, "You are going to the Presidential National Guard." You know what that means? You have to stand in front of the presidential palace in a box for eight hours or so, not blinking or moving. To me this would have been a death sentence. I heard some rumors that while many people last the entire twelve months or so, some people kill themselves because they couldn't take it anymore. It must've been so difficult.

I asked him why he was assigning me there. He replied saying that I was tall and skinny, and they were looking for people like me. I murmured, "Isn't that just my luck?" I had three to four months to get ready to join, so I decided to think really fast what I was going to do—go in to the army or leave the country. I had to make a decision.

Through a buddy at work I met a guy who could get me through the border easily. For a fee of course. I asked how, hoping that it wasn't through the water. He replied that it was on dry land, and if I did what he told me, I would be fine.

I was really hooked up but told him I didn't want to leave by myself. He happened to know two more guys who wanted to go too. So I went to meet them. My time was running short as I had until November to leave; otherwise, my dream would go down the drain. It was the beginning of October when we met, talked, and agreed to go on this journey together—Mr. Pavel, his son, Emanuel, and me.

Mr. Pavel was forty-seven or forty-eight years old. Emanuel was eighteen, and I was nineteen. I could not eat or sleep as I was always thinking about it. I was also scared. If they caught us, not only would they beat us really good, but we would also be thrown in prison.

For me it was more complicated. I already signed the application to join the army in Romania. I was to report November 10, 1984. If I did not, I was running from the army—being absent without official leave (AWOL)—and from the secret police. They would have done everything in their power to find me. Punishment would be imprisonment for a long time or working in a battalion, digging trenches at a Romanian canal. It was like signing your death certificate. It was a very tough decision, especially for a nineteen-year-old.

Time was passing really fast, and we agreed on a date. The three of us would go through with it. I went home, did some shopping (a suit, a tie, and a new pair of sneakers) because I knew I needed them to run while crossing the border. I had everything planned out. All we had to do was wait a few more days until the day that we set.

One morning I was waiting at a bus stop to go to work. I saw a guy driving a white American car, a Cadillac convertible. He had really long hair (you were not allowed to have long hair back then), and he was playing loud music. I think he must've been Romanian residing in the United States and was home visiting. We all looked at him like he was an angel dropped from the sky. To see something like that in those communist days was rare. You usually saw it only in the movies.

S eeing him gave me all the courage I needed. If he could do it, then I could do it, too, with God's help. So on November 9, the three of us left for Naides, a small village on the border with Yugoslavia and the hometown of the guy helping us cross over. When we got off at the last stop, border patrol were there, asking people the purposes of their visits. We got lucky; they didn't ask us anything. They were randomly checking the ones they thought were "odd."

The family we were staying with wanted me to marry their daughter. She was very pretty, but I did not consider it knowing what I was about to do.

We arrived late in the evening, and I told my companions we should go to the bar for a drink to celebrate going away and spending our last night in Romania. So we did. We drank a whole bottle of whiskey (Romanian brandy), went back home, and at 3:30 in the morning, we left toward the border, maybe twenty minutes of walking.

Everyone was asleep, and no one was on the road. That's what we wanted. I saw the border from twenty to twenty-five metres. We were all happy and scared at the same time. Full of adrenaline, my heart was beating pretty fast, and I told them this was it. We started crawling the twenty-five metres to not wake up the border patrol, who was still asleep at 3:50 in the morning. We passed the towers that they were watching from, and luckily, no one was in them.

W e ran toward the barbed-wire fence separating Romania and Yugoslavia. Before we got to the fence, I saw a trip wire shining out. The moon was huge in the sky, so the light reflected on the trip wire. I whispered at them to stop right away. I pointed at the wire and told them not to touch it. If we had, the trap would detonate flares, and it would have looked like daylight or the Fourth of July over here in America. The guards would wake up, let the dogs out, and start shooting at us; we would've been caught. But none of that happened. We started running fast and jumped the fence, which was about six or seven feet tall.

Emanuel and I got over the fence and ran over sixty metres. We stopped, and I noticed Mr. Pavel wasn't with us. I asked Emanuel where his dad was, but he didn't know. I looked back and saw him caught in the fence wire. We started hearing noises from the soldiers who were on to us. I told Emanuel we had to go back and get him, and he said to leave him there. I said, "No way. We came together, we leave together." So I went back, and he followed me. I grabbed his father really hard and pulled him out of the tangled wire, ripping his jacket apart. But the jacket didn't matter as long as he was free. We ran about a hundred metres. Being still dark outside, we were not sure we were on the right path until we saw a concrete marker, and written on it was, "Republic Socialist of Yugoslavia."

We were so happy to discover we were on the right path that we dropped to our knees and literally kissed the ground. We prayed, thanking God for helping us to cross safely and soundly.

As the three of us walked on the road, a bus came toward us. It passed by, but then it stopped ahead of us. We were so tired that we decided to run to the bus and let it take us wherever it was going. The bus backed up to us, and we got in. Three or four border police from Yugoslavia's side were aboard. They asked us to hand over our papers and identification cards. They kept them. They already knew—or at least suspected—we were Romanians, trespassing illegally into their country. After a while we stopped in a city and got out. Border patrol officers handcuffed us together and took us in to custody.

The next day they questioned us individually, asking what we were doing over there, where we wanted to go, and so on. I told one of them that I was a political refugee, and I wanted to go to Canada. He looked at me, smiled, and said, "No, you are going to the United States." I don't know why he chose where I should go. Maybe he had a good feeling about it. Of course I was very happy about going to America, and so were Mr. Pavel and Emanuel. But it would take more time to get there. After we gave them all the information, there was a lot of paperwork involved. Unfortunately, they took us to jail. We had to serve time, about two or three weeks, because we crossed illegally into their country.

Once we got to the city of Vršqc (Virsets), they gave us really short haircuts, threw some white powder on our heads, and fed us. I was so hungry—we hadn't eaten for days—that I went back for more. The jail was full of Romanian refugees just like us. Bunk beds were all over the room, and two or three people shared a bed.

There wasn't enough space, so I got the next best thing, a spot next to the toilet. I didn't sleep too much that night; I'll let you decide why not. In the morning, they told us that a lot of people were sent back to Romania but didn't know why. I never found out for sure, but my guess is the decision to send them back was based on information they got back from Romanian security, equivalent to the FBI in the United States.

It was tough knowing that after all we went through, we didn't know for sure if we were going forward. In those two to three weeks, they would decide if we were to be sent back or go forward. All we could do was wait and see.

In the meantime, they took us into a field to gather grapes since it was grape season. The time passed quickly, and I made a lot of new friends. Most of them were sent back in exchange for one train car full of salt per person. That's what the Romanian government was paying for each individual. Pretty sad.

At the end of the three weeks, my two buddies, two other guys, and I were loaded in a prison vehicle, and our fate was decided. I asked where they were taking us, but they wouldn't say a word. They drove us about an hour or so. I looked out a small window but couldn't see too much. The vehicle came to a stop, at what must've been a red light or a stop sign. Someone in the jail told us if it was the stop sign, they were making a right and would go straight to the Romanian border. If they made a left at the stop sign, we were going on the right path. We went left. We hugged each other, saying, "We made it. Thank God."

They drove us to Padinska-Skela. It wasn't a jail; it was more like a transit center. We spent two to three months there before going to Banja-Koviljaca. We sat there for a good while and took some English classes; pretty much everyone did. The last stop was to a hotel in the capital Belgrade. In our case, it was the Hotel Astoria. We had more freedom there. We could go into the city and to parks and movies. We could also work. Though room and board were free at the hotel, we needed pocket money.

After a while, we had an interview with the American Embassy. All we had to do was wait for an American sponsor. After so many months of waiting, I finally got a sponsor from New Windsor, Maryland.

My two buddies left before me for Seattle, Washington. I was to depart on the June 10, 1985. We got lucky, going to the United States in the relatively short time of eight months. Other people had to wait a year or more to go to the States. Prior to leaving, they gave us plane tickets, paid for by the sponsor, I believe. So on the tenth, I should be on the plane to Maryland.

That day came, and I said goodbye to my friends. I didn't have a suitcase or any money. All I had was a plastic bag containing my IDs and a change of clothes, I still have some of those clothes. By the way, that was me in the picture, taken few months prior leaving.

I had never flew on an airplane and was kind of scared. It ended up being quite a memorable adventure, and I enjoyed it. I arrived at the airport in New York, where they gave us vaccines—not sure for what—and a physical to make sure everything was okay.

All my friends went to different states, so we said goodbye and wished each other the best of luck. I had to catch a small plane to Maryland, where I stayed about a month. It was another transit center, where I had to wait for another sponsor. I got a sponsor from a Methodist church in Dallas, Texas. Everybody was saying I was going to a hot climate state and would have AC. I didn't know what AC meant until I got there. My sponsor's name was Jack. He gave me water and a pair of sunglasses on arrival. He was a very nice person. The next day, they took me to an agency and gave me a place to stay, some clothes, and a job.

My first job was at an apartment complex near Bachman Lake in Dallas. Among other things, I mowed grass and did a little painting. I was paid $4 an hour. It was enough at the time as rent was cheap and gas was under a dollar a gallon. Life was good.

In the previous picture are Emanuel and his dad, Mr. Pavel, the two guys I left Romania with.

After a while, I got a job as a machinist close to downtown Dallas. That's when I bought my first car, a 1977 Volvo 242 DL. I was very happy to have my own car. I was twenty-one when I got my driver's license and very proud.

Years passed, and I did some construction work up in Virginia with some friends of mine. That's when the Romanian government failed in 1989. I watched it on TV. Things were getting better in Eastern Europe. People had more freedom. Democracy changed the lives in many countries, and I was so happy about it.

In 1993 I returned home for the first time in almost ten years. My mom, rest in peace, was so happy to see me, and I to see her after many years apart. We started hugging, kissing, and crying each other. She kept telling me, "All this time I thought you were dead." I think that day, having me next to her, was the happiest day of her life.

I went back a few other times and then I got married in a church there to my wife, Ileana, on November 1997. After a couple months, she came over to the United States with a green card and all. Since I was an American citizen, it was pretty easy getting her over here quickly and legally.

Our first child was born on July 12, 1998, and we named our sweet daughter Madeline. Our son came along after three years, on December 14, 2001. He is my pride and joy. I'm really proud of them, but I'm especially proud of my wife for giving me such blessings. A daughter and a son, what more could you want? She put up with me all this time. I was not perfect, and we had our share of fights and suffering. You know it happens in marriage.

Whoever tells you that marriage is a bed of roses is lying. I know that for a fact. Sometimes we still fight for almost no reason. She still reminds me of what I did in the past. It's like she keeps count of it. I hope that someday she will forgive me fully.

I said I wouldn't write too much stuff about me. I don't want to bore you too much. If I did, I apologize.

What I'm about to write next is what happened to me on February 20, 2008. It is a true story.

Previous years I always got sick during the beginning of the year (January, February, March ...). I don't know, but this Texas weather is something else. I cut out the smoking and took better care of myself, so I usually got away with sickness pretty fast and with no major problems.

But this time was totally different. I was driving parts for Toyota. When I started feeling ill, I said to myself, "No worries. It will be like the previous year's, drink more water, hot tea several times a day, and it will all pass like before."

B ut boy was I wrong. I couldn't breathe well; I was dizzy and had no energy. So I dragged myself like that for couple of days, seeing no doctor whatsoever. On February 20, it got worse than before. My breathing became problematic. It was like I was breathing through a wet dust mask.

I knew from that moment it was going to be bad, like never before. So I stopped at a QT gas station, got some cold water and some Mentos to help me breathe easier. I started to drink water, but none of that worked. I felt the water come out of my mouth, I couldn't swallow it. I thought that my lungs were full of water, and that's why I couldn't breathe well.

I decided to go home to Allen, where I was living at the time, to see a doctor. I got close to home, driving on East McDermott Dr. toward Highway 5 (Greenville Ave.), and suddenly, I started breathing really hard, gasping for air. I slowed the truck down and slapped myself pretty hard on my face. I poured a lot of cold water on my head, thinking it would make me snap out of it and give me enough time to see a doctor.

B ut it only got worse by the second. I stopped my truck between the lanes to try and make a U-turn right in front of the Allen Cemetery. I told myself, "If anything happens to me, I do not want to hurt anyone else." I put my truck in park and left the engine running. My heart started to beat faster than ever before. I tried to breathe, but I couldn't. I was struggling. Then I started to get warm and felt a sensation of heat and calmness. I said to myself, "Oh, my, this is it." I knew at that moment I was going to die. I become disoriented felt my heart now beating very slowly. I had the sensation of getting pulled down, as though by a magnet, but felt warm and calm at the same time.

It's hard to explain that warmth. It was a kind of feeling that made me relaxed and feeling good in a very indescribable way. Then I let myself go because I could not hang on anymore. With my head facing down and almost touching the steering wheel, I felt someone's very warm hands slowly raise my head toward the ceiling of the truck. I don't know who it was, but he did it so gently. As I faced the truck's ceiling, in a split second the sky opened. I could see through the ceiling. There was a rectangular door in the sky with clouds around it. I went through the door and felt as if I was rapidly going through an upward tunnel filled with little stars. Then I ended up in what felt like the middle of the universe.

It was a strange place and very quiet. I felt like I was floating in the air. Then I saw a bright star coming toward me very fast. I looked at it coming my way, but when it got really close, I could not look at it anymore. It was very bright like; it was like looking at the sun for a time. I very slowly tilted my head to the left and away from it.

The surroundings were very strange to me. The sky around me looked grey, as if it was going to rain. All I could see in front of me was a white patch of cloud, maybe thirty feet wide and about sixty feet long. I don't know why, but I kept staring at it for a long time. Then I saw a staticky image of a man for a few seconds. He started walking toward me through the mist. He walked slowly, dragging his feet through the cloud as if walking through three feet of water. He was playing with his palms, waving his hands through the mist as he walked. Like how someone would roll down their windows in a car and do wave motions in the air. I wondered, *Who is he?* But somehow I knew. I felt as if he was a holy man. My first impression when seeing him for the first time was that he looked just like an owl.

When he got close, I could see his physical appearance. I was looking at him from above. I was about ten to fifteen feet above the clouds, looking down at him. Then he stood still. I could see him from the waist up. The rest of his body was covered by the clouds.

His skin tone was pale white, because his face was radiating light, enough to see his face clearly. He also had broad shoulders. He was wearing a cream cloak with a U-shaped neckline. He was staring at me, looking up at about a twenty-five-degree trajectory. He had wavy black hair that touched his shoulders. The style looked like thick dreads that were split, and his hairline wasn't parted. His beard was straight, and his hair in the front was short and touched the eyebrows. But they weren't thick like the rest of his hair; they were wavier and thinner. The beard was also black, not very thick on the sides, and it was longer on the chin by about half an inch. He had a braid around his forehead, as if wearing a headband. But it wasn't on top of his hair; it was under. His nose was hooked in a v shape, facing downward, and the tip of the nose was very skinny. He had hazel eyes, rounded eyebrows, and skinny lips. The things that surprised me the most were his eyes. His eyes were hazel in color and had large black pupils. But his eyes were large, like owl size. No human being had eyes like his. I never saw anything like that on any person. I felt so at peace and so warm just by looking at him.

Why was I looking downward at him? I don't know. I couldn't look to my left or right or where I was standing. Nothing of that sort. It was like he made me look at him only. Period.

He made very slow movements, looking at my left and then directly at me. At the same time, I saw him shake his head hesitantly, like he had doubts about me about something. Only he knew what was he thinking. My guess was that he was trying to decide whether to give me more time on earth to do what I was supposed to do or take me with him. When he shook his head like that, it looked very funny. He did that about three times. Then I wondered, *What's he doing?* in English.

I couldn't see his hands or his feet, but I felt for sure that he was God, our Maker. I had no doubt about that. Then I saw a strong, powerful ray of light shine from my left toward him. The Bible would say it was the transfiguration. Then he turned to the side, closed his eyes, and looked upward. I saw his tunic and face become very bright, but his hair looked normal, black and shiny. I remember that very well; it looked like when someone puts a powerful flashlight toward you from above at an angle in the dark.

hen I saw his profile so close, as though he was holding me in his arms. I kept looking at his beard while he was looking away. I could not look wherever he was looking. Again, I don't know why. It was as if he wouldn't let me. That was the last thing I remember.

Though I have no idea how long I was dead, I am sure that's what happened. It felt like three minutes on earth but longer in heaven. I woke up still facing upward, but I could breathe better. When I looked to my right, I could see the traffic coming from the east side standing still. It was as if there was a red light, but there wasn't. Traffic was about fifty feet from where I was in my truck. I wondered why none of the vehicles in those lanes didn't move. It felt weird. The cars then started to roll. I put my truck in gear and went to the nearby family clinic.

The doctor checked me out, and I told him about my problem. He gave me some antibiotics, insisting that I take them as soon as I got them from the pharmacy. He seemed more scared than I was. I think he saw that I was in bad shape. I'd like to think he saved my life. That's why he's still my doctor to this day.

I t took me quite a while to get back on my feet; I wasn't out of the woods yet. I remember, the next day I was a totally changed man. It felt like when I had my first-born child. To tell you the truth, I didn't want people to look at me like I was crazy, as if I had lost my marbles. I'm the kind of guy that likes to keep to himself. It's better than being laughed at.

I have listened to the Christian radio ever since then. I encourage you to do so as well. It was a very knowledgeable radio program. I learned a lot about the Bible and day-by-day life.

Since then, I think about Him every day. Not a day goes by where I don't think of Him. After a while, I thought to myself, maybe that's why God let me spend more time on this Earth—to talk about Him so that you may believe in Him.

That's the reason I started writing this book—so that more people can change their hearts and truly believe in God.

Before I wrote this book, only about twelve to thirteen people knew about it, including my wife, my children, my sister, and some friends of mine. Hopefully many more will read about it.

I know that a lot of you will question me about dying. It felt peaceful. It didn't feel bad at all; actually, it felt good. You feel that heavenly warmth, and then you start to relax. You feel like you have to let go of yourself, and there's nothing you can do about it.

I remember someone on the Christian radio said, "Missing from this body means to be present with the Lord," and that's the truth.

All I'm saying is that everyone has a certain time on this earth, so live it fully, be happy, trust in God with all your heart, pray, and be kind to each other. Like I wrote here, there is life after death, and I hope from the bottom of my heart that when your time comes, you will be in heaven just by believing, truly believing in God, the only God,

Jesus Christ, Amen.

Be kind to one another, tenderhearted, forgiving each other, as God in Christ also has forgiven you. (Ephesians 4:32 NASB)

Printed in the United States
by Baker & Taylor Publisher Services